THE FIRST BOOK OF URIZEN

William Blake

Table of Contents

THE FIRST BOOK OF URIZEN

William Blake

Kessinger Publishing reprints thousands of hard–to–find books!

Visit us at http://www.kessinger.net

Preludium to the First Book of Urizen

Of the primeval Priest's assum'd power,
When Eternals spurn'd back his Religion,
And gave him a place in the North,
Obscure, shadowy, void, solitary.

Eternals! I hear your call gladly.
Dictate swift wingèd words, and fear not
To unfold your dark visions of torment.

CHAPTER I

1. Lo, a Shadow of horror is risen
In Eternity! unknown, unprolific,
Self–clos'd, all–repelling. What Demon
Hath form'd this abominable Void,
This soul–shudd'ring Vacuum? Some said
It is Urizen. But unknown, abstracted,
Brooding, secret, the dark Power hid.

2. Times on times he divided, and measur'd
Space by space in his ninefold darkness,
Unseen, unknown; changes appear'd
Like desolate mountains, rifted furious
By the black winds of perturbation.

3. For he strove in battles dire,
In unseen conflictions with Shapes,
Bred from his forsaken wilderness,
Of beast, bird, fish, serpent, and element,
Combustion, blast, vapour, and cloud.

4. Dark, revolving in silent activity,
Unseen in tormenting passions,
An Activity unknown and horrible,
A self–contemplating Shadow,
In enormous labours occupièd.

5. But Eternals beheld his vast forests;
Ages on ages he lay, clos'd, unknown,
Brooding, shut in the deep; all avoid
The petrific, abominable Chaos.

6. His cold horrors, silent, dark Urizen
Prepar'd; his ten thousands of thunders,

THE FIRST BOOK OF URIZEN

Rang'd in gloom'd array, stretch out across
The dread world; and the rolling of wheels,
As of swelling seas, sound in his clouds,

In his hills of stor'd snows, in his mountains
Of hail and ice; voices of terror
Are heard, like thunders of autumn,
When the cloud blazes over the harvests.

CHAPTER II

1. Earth was not, nor globes of attraction;
The will of the Immortal expanded
Or contracted his all–flexible senses;
Death was not, but Eternal life sprung.

2. The sound of a trumpet the heavens
Awoke, and vast clouds of blood roll'd
Round the dim rocks of Urizen, so nam'd
That solitary one in Immensity.

3. Shrill the trumpet! and myriads of Eternity
Muster around the bleak deserts,
Now fill'd with clouds, darkness, and waters,
That roll'd perplex'd, lab'ring; and utter'd
Words articulate, bursting in thunders,
That roll'd on the tops of his mountains:—

4. `From the depths of dark solitude, from
The Eternal abode in my Holiness,
Hidden, set apart, in my stern counsels,
Reserv'd for the days of futurity,
I have sought for a joy without pain,
For a solid without fluctuation.
Why will you die, O Eternals?
Why live in unquenchable burnings?

5. `First I fought with the fire, consum'd
Inwards into a deep world within,
A Void immense, wild, dark and deep,
Where nothing was—Nature's wide womb;
And self–balanc'd, stretch'd o'er the void,
I alone, even I! the winds merciless
Bound; but condensing in torrents

They fall and fall; strong I repell'd
The vast waves, and arose on the waters
A wide World of solid obstruction.

6. `Here alone I, in books form'd of metals,
Have written the secrets of Wisdom,
The secrets of dark Contemplation,
By fightings and conflicts dire
With terrible monsters sin–bred,
Which the bosoms of all inhabit—
Seven deadly Sins of the Soul.

7. `Lo! I unfold my darkness, and on
This rock place, with strong hand, the Book
Of Eternal brass, written in my solitude:

8. `Laws of peace, of love, of unity,
Of pity, compassion, forgiveness;
Let each choose one habitation,
His ancient infinite mansion,
One command, one joy, one desire,
One curse, one weight, one measure,
One King, one God, one Law.'

CHAPTER III

1. The voice ended: they saw his pale visage
Emerge from the darkness, his hand
On the rock of Eternity unclasping
The Book of brass. Rage seiz'd the strong—

2. Rage, fury, intense indignation,
In cataracts of fire, blood, and gall,
In whirlwinds of sulphurous smoke,
And enormous forms of energy,
In living creations appear'd,
In the flames of eternal fury.

3. Sund'ring, dark'ning, thund'ring,
Rent away with a terrible crash,
Eternity roll'd wide apart,
Wide asunder rolling;
Mountainous, all around
Departing, departing, departing,
Leaving ruinous fragments of life,
Hanging, frowning cliffs, and, all between,
An Ocean of voidness unfathomable.

4. The roaring fires ran o'er the heav'ns
In whirlwinds and cataracts of blood,
And o'er the dark deserts of Urizen
Fires pour thro' the void, on all sides,
On Urizen's self—begotten armies.

5. But no light from the fires! all was darkness
In the flames of Eternal fury.

6. In fierce anguish and quenchless flames
To the deserts and rocks he ran raging,

To hide; but he could not. Combining,
He dug mountains and hills in vast strength,
He pilèd them in incessant labour,
In howlings and pangs and fierce madness,
Long periods in burning fires labouring;
Till hoary, and age–broke, and agèd,
In despair and the shadows of death

7. And a roof vast, petrific, around
On all sides he fram'd, like a womb,
Where thousands of rivers, in veins
Of blood, pour down the mountains to cool
The eternal fires, beating without
From Eternals; and like a black Globe,
View'd by sons of Eternity, standing
On the shore of the infinite ocean,
Like a human heart, struggling and beating,
The vast world of Urizen appear'd.

8. And Los, round the dark globe of Urizen,
Kept watch for Eternals to confine
The obscure separation alone;
For Eternity stood wide apart,
As the stars are apart from the earth,

9. Los wept, howling around the dark Demon,
And cursing his lot; for in anguish
Urizen was rent from his side,
And a fathomless Void for his feet,
And intense fires for his dwelling.

10. But Urizen, laid in a story sleep,
Unorganiz'd, rent from Eternity.

11. The Eternals said: `What is this? Death?
Urizen is a clod of clay!'

12. Los howl'd in a dismal stupor,
Groaning, gnashing, groaning,
Till the wrenching apart was healèd.

13. But the wrenching of Urizen heal'd not.
Cold, featureless, flesh or clay,
Rifted with direful changes,
He lay in a dreamless night,

14. Till Los rous'd his fires, affrighted
At the formless, unmeasurable Death.

CHAPTER IV

1. Los, smitten with astonishment,
Frighten'd at the hurtling bones

2. And at the surging, sulphureous,
Perturbèd, immortal, mad raging

3. In whirlwinds, and pitch, and nitre
Round the furious limbs of Los.

4. And Los formèd nets and gins,
And threw the nets round about.

5. He watch'd in shudd'ring fear
The dark changes, and bound every change
With rivets of iron and brass.

6. And these were the changes of Urizen:—

CHAPTER IV A

1. Ages on ages roll'd over him;
In stony sleep ages roll'd over him,
Like a dark waste stretching, changeable,
By earthquakes riv'n, belching sullen fires:
On ages roll'd ages in ghastly
Sick torment; around him in whirlwinds
Of darkness the Eternal Prophet howl'd,
Beating still on his rivets of iron,
Pouring solder of iron; dividing
The horrible night into watches.

2. And Urizen (so his eternal name)
His prolific delight obscur'd more and more,
In dark secrecy hiding in surging
Sulphureous fluid his phantasies.
The Eternal Prophet heav'd the dark bellows,
And turn'd restless the tongs, and the hammer
Incessant beat, forging chains new and new,
Numb'ring with links hours, days, and years.

3. The Eternal mind, bounded, began to roll
Eddies of wrath, ceaseless, round and round,
And the sulphureous foam, surging thick,
Settled, a lake, bright and shining clear,
White as the snow on the mountains cold.

4. Forgetfulness, dumbness, necessity,
In chains of the mind lockèd up,
Like fetters of ice shrinking together,
Disorganiz'd, rent from Eternity,
Los beat on his fetters of iron;
And heated his furnaces, and pour'd
Iron solder and solder of brass.

5. Restless turn'd the Immortal, enchain'd,
Heaving dolorous, anguish'd, unbearable;
Till a roof, shaggy, wild, enclos'd
In an orb his fountain of thought.

6. In a horrible, dreamful slumber,
Like the linkèd infernal chain,
A vast Spine writh'd in torment
Upon the winds, shooting pain'd
Ribs, like a bending cavern;
And bones of solidness froze
Over all his nerves of joy—
And a first Age passèd over,
And a state of dismal woe.

7. From the caverns of his jointed Spine
Down sunk with fright a red
Round Globe, hot, burning, deep,
Deep down into the Abyss;
Panting, conglobing, trembling,
Shooting out ten thousand branches
Around his solid bones—
And a second Age passèd over,
And a state of dismal woe.

8. In harrowing fear rolling round,
His nervous Brain shot branches
Round the branches of his Heart,
On high, into two little orbs,
And fixèd in two little caves,
Hiding carefully from the wind,
His Eyes beheld the deep—
And a third Age passèd over,
And a state of dismal woe.

9. The pangs of hope began.
In heavy pain, striving, struggling,
Two Ears, in close volutions,
From beneath his orbs of vision
Shot spiring out, and petrified
As they grew—And a fourth Age passèd,
And a state of dismal woe.

10. In ghastly torment sick,
Hanging upon the wind,
Two Nostrils bent down to the deep—
And a fifth Age passèd over,
And a state of dismal woe.

11. In ghastly torment sick,
Within his ribs bloated round
A craving, hungry Cavern;
Thence arose his channell'd Throat,
And, like a red flame, a Tongue
Of thirst and of hunger appear'd—
And a sixth Age passèd over,
And a state of dismal woe.

12. Enragèd and stifled with torment,
He threw his right Arm to the North,
His left Arm to the South,
Shooting out in anguish deep,
And his Feet stamp'd the nether Abyss
In trembling and howling and dismay—
And a seventh Age passèd over,
And a state of dismal woe.

CHAPTER V

1. In terrors Los shrunk from his task:
His great hammer fell from his hand;
His fires beheld, and sickening
Hid their strong limbs in smoke;
For with noises, ruinous, loud,
With hurtlings and clashings and groans,
The Immortal endur'd his chains,
Tho' bound in a deadly sleep.

2. All the myriads of Eternity,
All the wisdom and joy of life
Roll like a sea around him;
Except what his little orbs
Of sight by degrees unfold.

3. And now his Eternal life,
Like a dream, was obliterated.

4. Shudd'ring, the Eternal Prophet smote
With a stroke from his North to South region.
The bellows and hammer are silent now;
A nerveless silence his prophetic voice
Seiz'd; a cold Solitude and dark Void
The Eternal Prophet and Urizen clos'd.

5. Ages on ages roll'd over them,
Cut off from life and light, frozen
Into horrible forms of deformity.
Los suffer'd his fires to decay;
Then he look'd back with anxious desire,
But the Space, undivided by existence,
Struck horror into his soul.

6. Los wept, obscur'd with mourning,
His bosom earthquak'd with sighs;
He saw Urizen, deadly, black,
In his chains bound; and Pity began,

7. In anguish dividing and dividing—
For Pity divides the soul—
In pangs, Eternity on Eternity,
Life in cataracts pour'd down his cliffs.
The Void shrunk the lymph into Nerves,
Wand'ring wide on the bosom of night,
And left a round globe of blood
Trembling upon the Void.
Thus the Eternal Prophet was divided
Before the death image of Urizen;
For in changeable clouds and darkness,
In a winterly night beneath,
The Abyss of Los stretch'd immense;
And now seen, now obscur'd, to the eyes
Of Eternals the visions remote
Of the dark separation appear'd:
As glasses discover Worlds
In the endless Abyss of space,
So the expanding eyes of Immortals
Beheld the dark visions of Los,
And the globe of life–blood trembling.

8. The globe of life–blood trembled,
Branching out into roots,
Fibrous, writhing upon the winds,
Fibres of blood, milk, and tears,
In pangs, Eternity on Eternity.
At length in tears and cries embodièd,
A Female form, trembling and pale,
Waves before his deathy face.

9. All Eternity shudder'd at sight
Of the first Female, now separate,
Pale as a cloud of snow,
Waving before the face of Los.

10. Wonder, awe, fear, astonishment
Petrify the Eternal myriads
At the first Female form now separate.
They call'd her Pity, and fled.

11. `Spread a Tent with strong curtains around them!
Let cords and stakes bind in the Void,
That Eternals may no more behold them.'

12. They began to weave curtains of darkness,
They erected large pillars round the Void,
With golden hooks fasten'd in the pillars;
With infinite labour the Eternals
A woof wove, and callèd it Science.

CHAPTER VI

1. But Los saw the Female, and pitièd;
He embrac'd her; she wept, she refus'd;
In perverse and cruel delight
She fled from his arms, yet he follow'd.

2. Eternity shudder'd when they saw
Man begetting his likeness
On his own Divided Image!

3. A time passèd over: the Eternals
Began to erect the tent,
When Enitharmon, sick,
Felt a Worm within her womb.

4. Yet helpless it lay, like a Worm
In the trembling womb,
To be moulded into existence.

5. All day the Worm lay on her bosom;
All night within her womb
The Worm lay till it grew to a Serpent,
With dolorous hissings and poisons
Round Enitharmon's loins folding.

6. Coil'd within Enitharmon's womb
The Serpent grew, casting its scales;
With sharp pangs the hissings began

To change to a grating cry —
Many sorrows and dismal throes,
Many forms of fish, bird, and beast
Brought forth an Infant form
Where was a Worm before.

7. The Eternals their tent finishèd,
Alarm'd with these gloomy visions,
When Enitharmon, groaning,
Produc'd a Man–Child to the light.

8. A shriek ran thro' Eternity,
And a paralytic stroke,
At the birth of the Human Shadow.

9. Delving earth in his resistless way,
Howling, the Child with fierce flames
Issu'd from Enitharmon.

10. The Eternals closèd the tent;
They beat down the stakes, the cords
Stretch'd for a work of Eternity —
No more Los beheld Eternity!

11. In his hands he seiz'd the Infant,
He bathèd him in springs of sorrow,
He gave him to Enitharmon.

CHAPTER VII

1. They namèd the child Orc; he grew,
Fed with milk of Enitharmon.

2. Los awoke her. O sorrow and pain!
A tight'ning girdle grew
Around his bosom. In sobbings
He burst the girdle in twain;
But still another girdle
Oppress'd his bosom. In sobbings

Again he burst it. Again
Another girdle succeeds.
The girdle was form'd by day;
By night was burst in twain.

3. These falling down on the Rock
Into an iron Chain,
In each other link by link lock'd.

4. They took Orc to the top of a mountain.
O how Enitharmon wept!
They chain'd his young limbs to the Rock
With the Chain of Jealousy,
Beneath Urizen's deathful Shadow.

5. The Dead heard the voice of the Child,
And began to awake from sleep;
All things heard the voice of the Child,
And began to awake to life.

6. And Urizen, craving with hunger,
Stung with the odours of Nature,
Explor'd his dens around.

7. He form'd a line and a plummet
To divide the Abyss beneath;
He form'd a dividing rule;

8. He formèd scales to weigh,
He formèd massy weights;
He formèd a brazen quadrant;
He formèd golden compasses,
And began to explore the Abyss;
And he planted a garden of fruits.

9. But Los encircled Enitharmon
With fires of Prophecy
From the sight of Urizen and Orc.

10. And she bore an enormous race.

CHAPTER VIII

1. Urizen explor'd his dens,
Mountain, moor, and wilderness,
With a globe of fire lighting his journey —
A fearful journey, annoy'd
By cruel enormities, forms
Of life on his forsaken mountains.

2. And his World teem'd vast enormities,
Fright'ning, faithless, fawning,
Portions of life, similitudes
Of a foot, or a hand, or a head,
Or a heart, or an eye; they swam mischievous,
Dread terrors, delighting in blood!

3. Most Urizen sicken'd to see
His eternal creations appear,
Sons and daughters of sorrow, on mountains,
Weeping, wailing. First Thiriel appear'd,
Astonish'd at his own existence,
Like a man from a cloud born; and Utha,
From the waters emerging, laments;
Grodna rent the deep earth, howling,
Amaz'd; his heavens immense crack
Like the ground parch'd with heat; then Fuzon
Flam'd out, first begotten, last born;
All his Eternal sons in like manner;
His daughters, from green herbs and cattle,
From monsters and worms of the pit.

4. He in darkness clos'd view'd all his race,
And his soul sicken'd! He curs'd
Both sons and daughters; for he saw
That no flesh nor spirit could keep

His iron laws one moment.

5. For he saw that Life liv'd upon Death:
The Ox in the slaughter–house moans;
The Dog at the wintry door;
And he wept, and he callèd it Pity,
And his tears flowèd down on the winds.

6. Cold he wander'd on high, over their Cities,
In weeping and pain and woe;
And wherever he wander'd, in sorrows
Upon the agèd Heavens,
A cold Shadow follow'd behind him
Like a spider's web, moist, cold, and dim,
Drawing out from his sorrowing soul,
The dungeon–like heaven dividing,
Wherever the footsteps of Urizen
Walkèd over the cities in sorrow;

7. Till a Web, dark and cold, throughout all
The tormented element stretch'd
From the sorrows of Urizen's soul.
And the Web is a Female in embryo;
None could break the Web, no wings of fire,

8. So twisted the cords, and so knotted
The meshes, twisted like to the human brain.

9. And all call'd it the Net of Religion.

CHAPTER IX

1. Then the Inhabitants of those Cities
Felt their Nerves change into Marrow,
And hardening Bones began
In swift diseases and torments,
In throbbings and shootings and grindings,
Thro' all the coasts; till weaken'd
The Senses inward rush'd, shrinking
Beneath the dark Net of infection;

2. Till the shrunken eyes, clouded over,
Discern'd not the woven Hypocrisy;
But the streaky slime in their heavens,
Brought together by narrowing perceptions,
Appear'd transparent air; for their eyes
Grew small like the eyes of a man,
And, in reptile forms shrinking together,
Of seven feet stature they remain'd.

3. Six days they shrunk up from existence,
And on the seventh day they rested,
And they bless'd the seventh day, in sick hope,
And forgot their Eternal life.

4. And their Thirty Cities divided
In form of a Human Heart.
No more could they rise at will
In the infinite Void, but bound down
To earth by their narrowing perceptions,
They livèd a period of years;
Then left a noisome body
To the jaws of devouring darkness.

5. And their children wept, and built

Tombs in the desolate places,
And form'd Laws of Prudence, and call'd them
The Eternal Laws of God.

6. And the Thirty Cities remain'd,
Surrounded by salt floods, now call'd
Africa: its name was then Egypt.

7. The remaining sons of Urizen
Beheld their brethren shrink together
Beneath the Net of Urizen.
Persuasion was in vain;
For the ears of the inhabitants
Were wither'd and deafen'd and cold,
And their eyes could not discern
Their brethren of other cities.

8. So Fuzon call'd all together
The remaining children of Urizen,
And they left the pendulous earth.
They callèd it Egypt, and left it.

9. And the salt Ocean rollèd englob'd.